JR. GRAPHIC MYTHS: GREEK HEROES

Achilles and the Trojan War

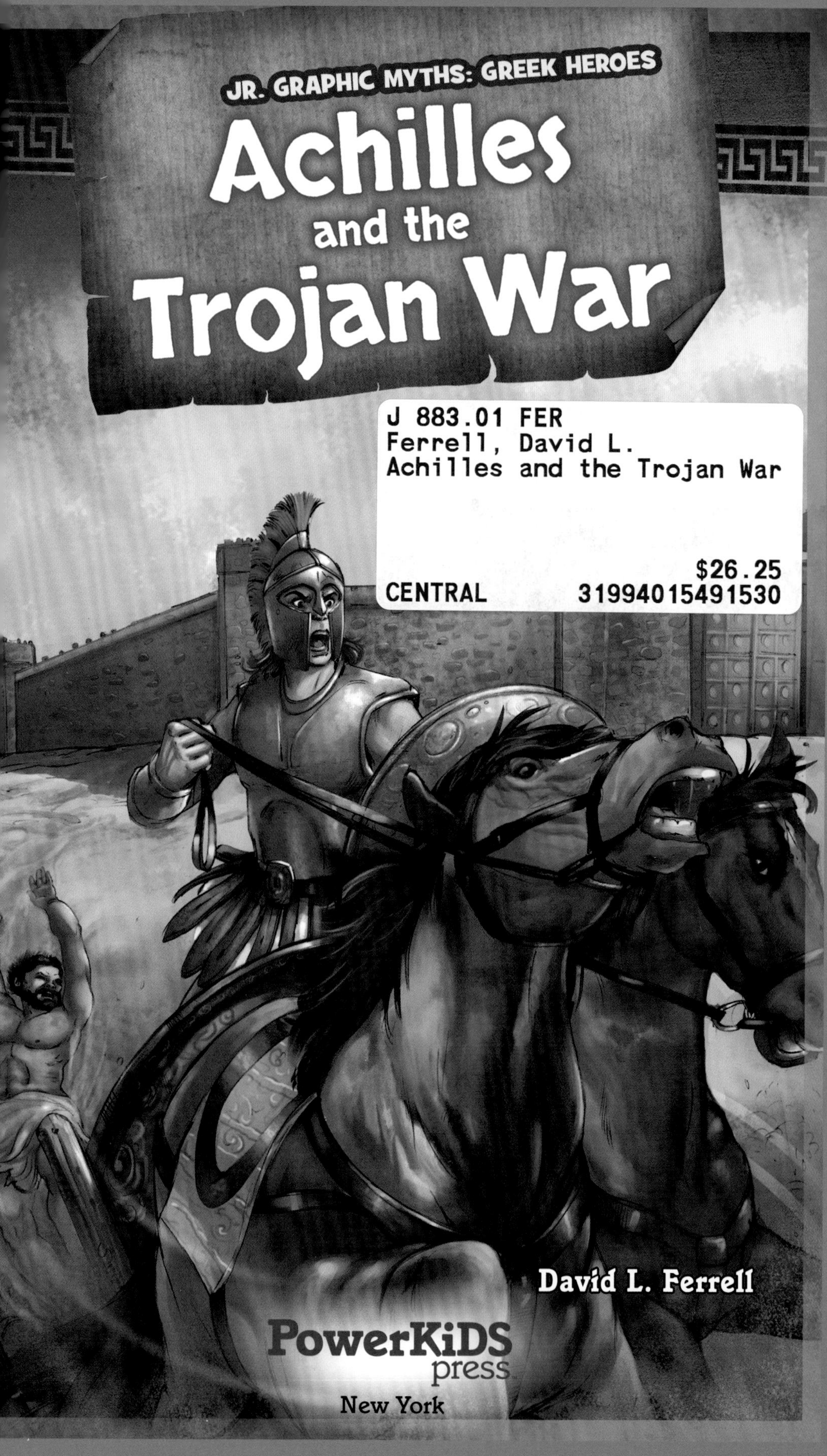

David L. Ferrell

PowerKiDS press
New York

Published in 2014 by The Rosen Publishing Group, Inc.
29 East 21st Street, New York, NY 10010

First Edition

Editor: Joanne Randolph
Book Design: Contentra Technologies
Illustrations: Contentra Technologies

Publisher's Cataloging Data

Ferrell, David L.
Achilles and the Trojan War / by David L. Ferrell. — First Edition.
    p. cm. — (Jr. graphic myths: Greek heroes)
Includes index.
ISBN 978-1-4777-6240-0 (library binding) — ISBN 978-1-4777-6241-7 (pbk.) — ISBN 978-1-4777-6242-4 (6-pack)
1. Achilles (Greek mythology) — Juvenile literature. 2. Trojan War — Juvenile literature. I. Title.
BL820.A22 F47 2014
398.20938—d23

Manufactured in the United States of America
CPSIA Compliance Information: Batch #W14PK1: For Further Information contact Rosen Publishing, New York, New York at 1-800-237-9932

Contents

Introduction

The writings of ancient Greece are filled with myths about epic battles, meddlesome gods, passionate romances, poets, monsters, and more. This is the story of Achilles, the legendary warrior of ancient Greece. When Paris, the **Trojan** prince, kidnapped Helen, the Greek armies joined together under the great king Agamemnon to bring her back. The **Achaean** Greeks would fight the Trojans for 10 years. Agamemnon's pride, however, would threaten to destroy the Achaeans' chances of victory. When he took Achilles' battle prize, Achilles refused to fight, but only Achilles could stand against the fearsome Trojan warrior Hector.

Main Characters

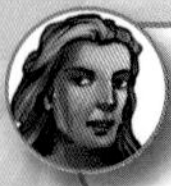

Achilles Champion of the Achaean army. Son of Peleus, a mortal man, and Thetis, a goddess of the sea.

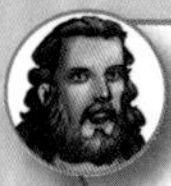

Agamemnon Leader of the Achaeans. Brother of Menelaus, the king of Sparta.

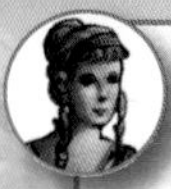

Helen Wife of Menelaus, king of Sparta. Kidnapped by Paris and taken to Troy. The Achaeans go to war with the Trojans to get her back.

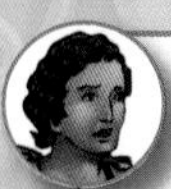

Paris Son of King Priam of Troy. **Abductor** of Helen, the wife of Menelaus.

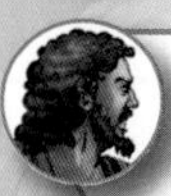

Hector Son of King Priam of Troy. Champion of the Trojan army.

Achilles and the Trojan War

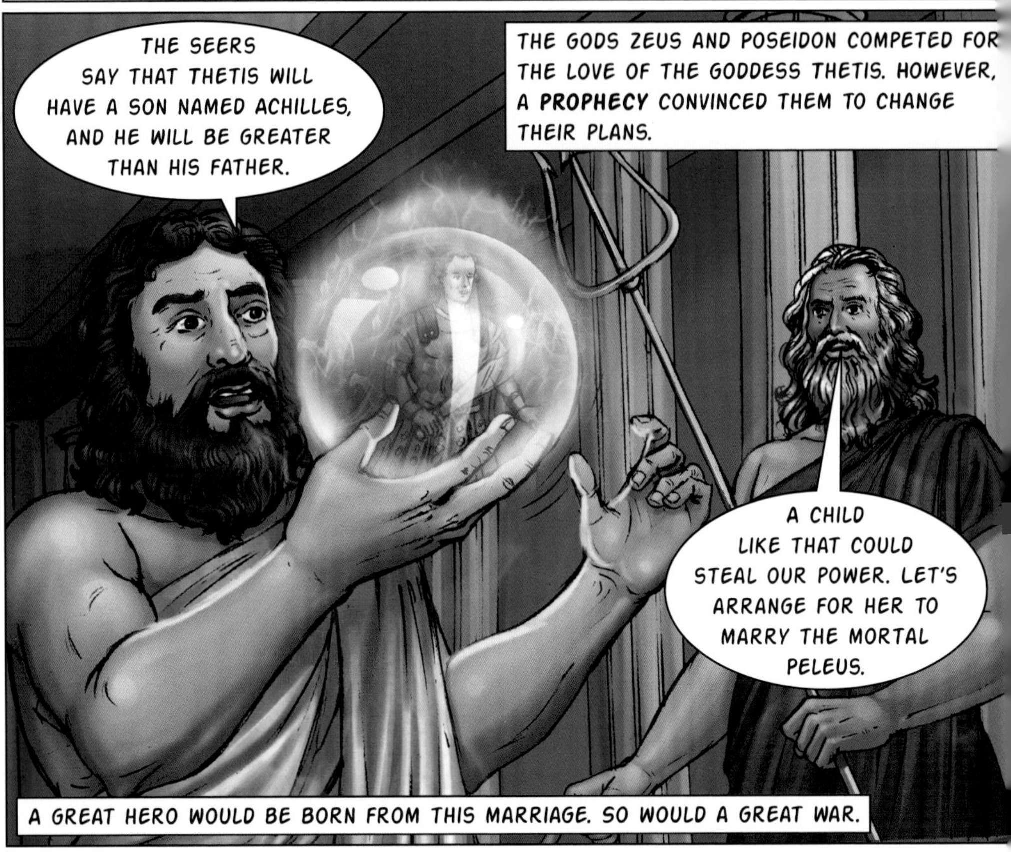
THE GODS ZEUS AND POSEIDON COMPETED FOR THE LOVE OF THE GODDESS THETIS. HOWEVER, A **PROPHECY** CONVINCED THEM TO CHANGE THEIR PLANS.
THE SEERS SAY THAT THETIS WILL HAVE A SON NAMED ACHILLES, AND HE WILL BE GREATER THAN HIS FATHER.
A CHILD LIKE THAT COULD STEAL OUR POWER. LET'S ARRANGE FOR HER TO MARRY THE MORTAL PELEUS.
A GREAT HERO WOULD BE BORN FROM THIS MARRIAGE. SO WOULD A GREAT WAR.

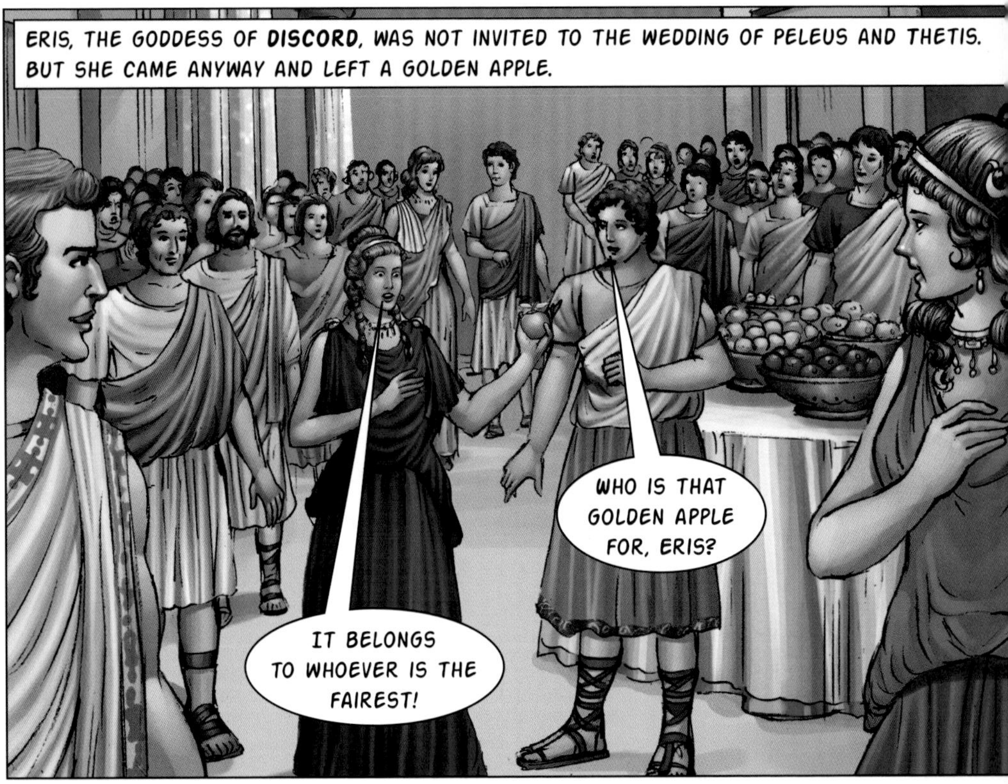
ERIS, THE GODDESS OF **DISCORD**, WAS NOT INVITED TO THE WEDDING OF PELEUS AND THETIS. BUT SHE CAME ANYWAY AND LEFT A GOLDEN APPLE.
WHO IS THAT GOLDEN APPLE FOR, ERIS?
IT BELONGS TO WHOEVER IS THE FAIREST!

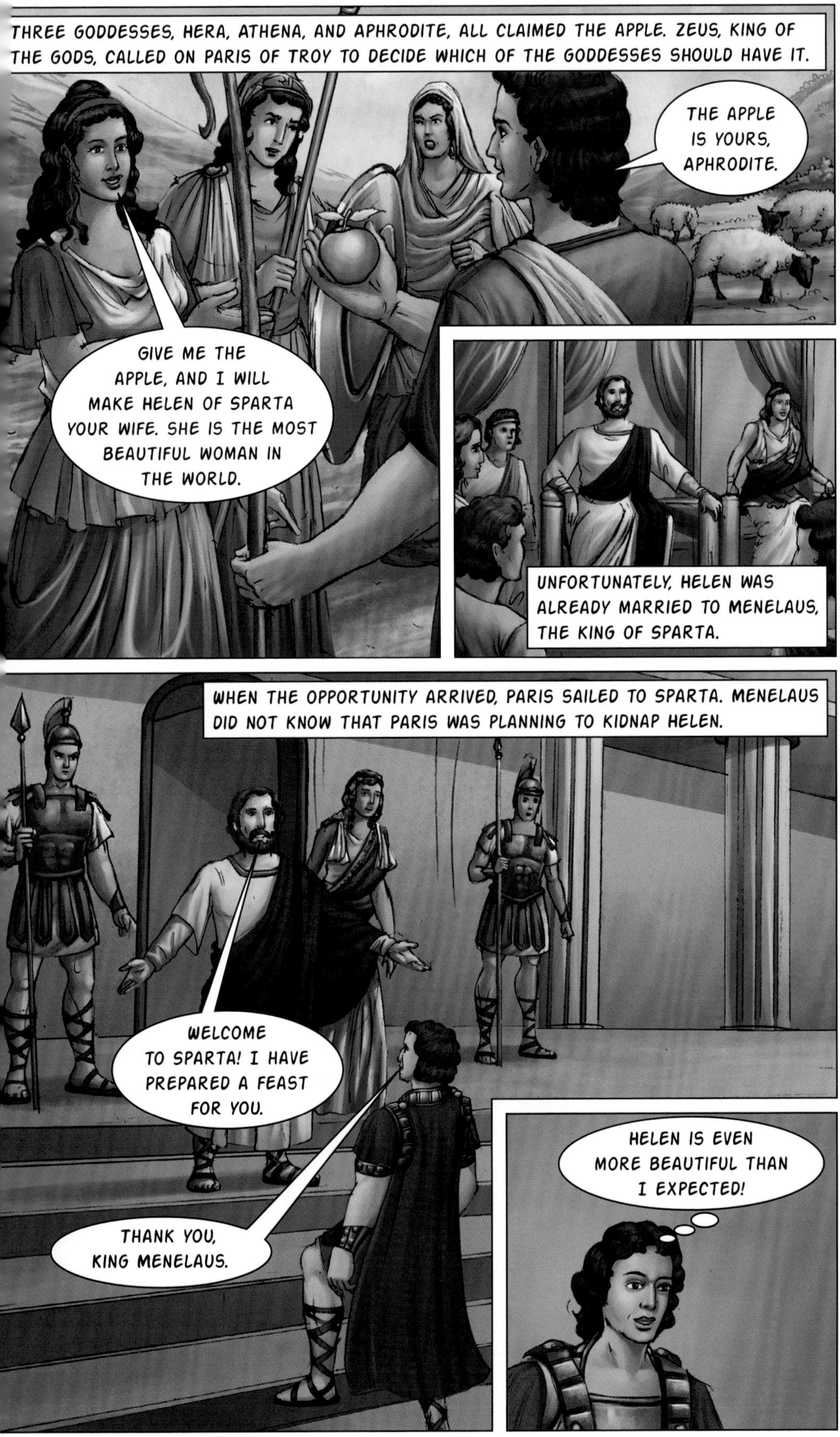
THREE GODDESSES, HERA, ATHENA, AND APHRODITE, ALL CLAIMED THE APPLE. ZEUS, KING OF THE GODS, CALLED ON PARIS OF TROY TO DECIDE WHICH OF THE GODDESSES SHOULD HAVE IT.
GIVE ME THE APPLE, AND I WILL MAKE HELEN OF SPARTA YOUR WIFE. SHE IS THE MOST BEAUTIFUL WOMAN IN THE WORLD.
THE APPLE IS YOURS, APHRODITE.
UNFORTUNATELY, HELEN WAS ALREADY MARRIED TO MENELAUS, THE KING OF SPARTA.
WHEN THE OPPORTUNITY ARRIVED, PARIS SAILED TO SPARTA. MENELAUS DID NOT KNOW THAT PARIS WAS PLANNING TO KIDNAP HELEN.
WELCOME TO SPARTA! I HAVE PREPARED A FEAST FOR YOU.
THANK YOU, KING MENELAUS.
HELEN IS EVEN MORE BEAUTIFUL THAN I EXPECTED!

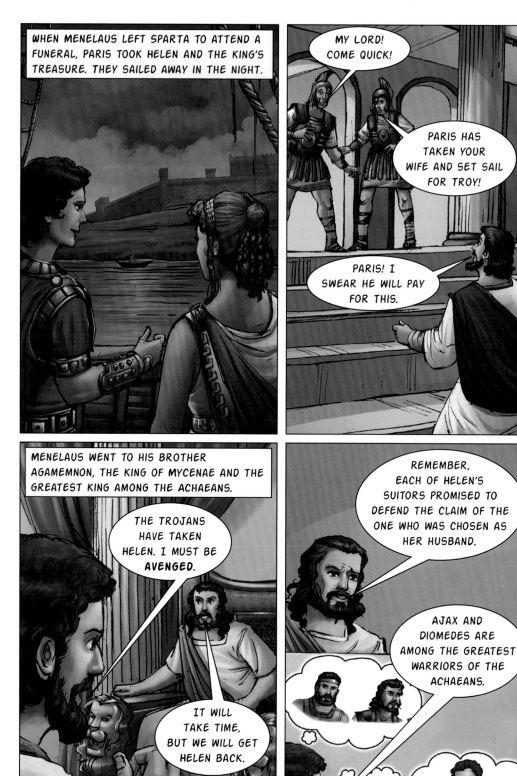

WHEN MENELAUS LEFT SPARTA TO ATTEND A FUNERAL, PARIS TOOK HELEN AND THE KING'S TREASURE. THEY SAILED AWAY IN THE NIGHT.

MY LORD! COME QUICK!

PARIS HAS TAKEN YOUR WIFE AND SET SAIL FOR TROY!

PARIS! I SWEAR HE WILL PAY FOR THIS.

MENELAUS WENT TO HIS BROTHER AGAMEMNON, THE KING OF MYCENAE AND THE GREATEST KING AMONG THE ACHAEANS.

THE TROJANS HAVE TAKEN HELEN. I MUST BE AVENGED.

IT WILL TAKE TIME, BUT WE WILL GET HELEN BACK.

REMEMBER, EACH OF HELEN'S SUITORS PROMISED TO DEFEND THE CLAIM OF THE ONE WHO WAS CHOSEN AS HER HUSBAND.

AJAX AND DIOMEDES ARE AMONG THE GREATEST WARRIORS OF THE ACHAEANS.

ODYSSEUS IS A CUNNING MAN.

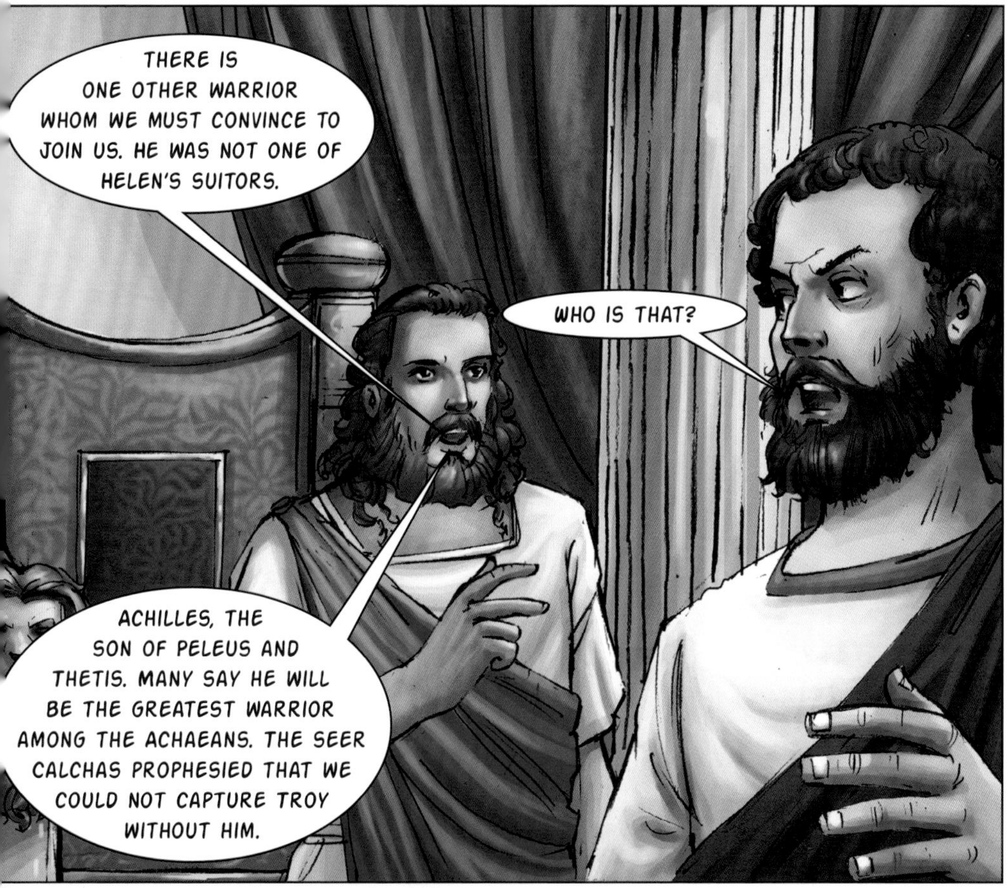
THERE IS ONE OTHER WARRIOR WHOM WE MUST CONVINCE TO JOIN US. HE WAS NOT ONE OF HELEN'S SUITORS.
WHO IS THAT?
ACHILLES, THE SON OF PELEUS AND THETIS. MANY SAY HE WILL BE THE GREATEST WARRIOR AMONG THE ACHAEANS. THE SEER CALCHAS PROPHESIED THAT WE COULD NOT CAPTURE TROY WITHOUT HIM.

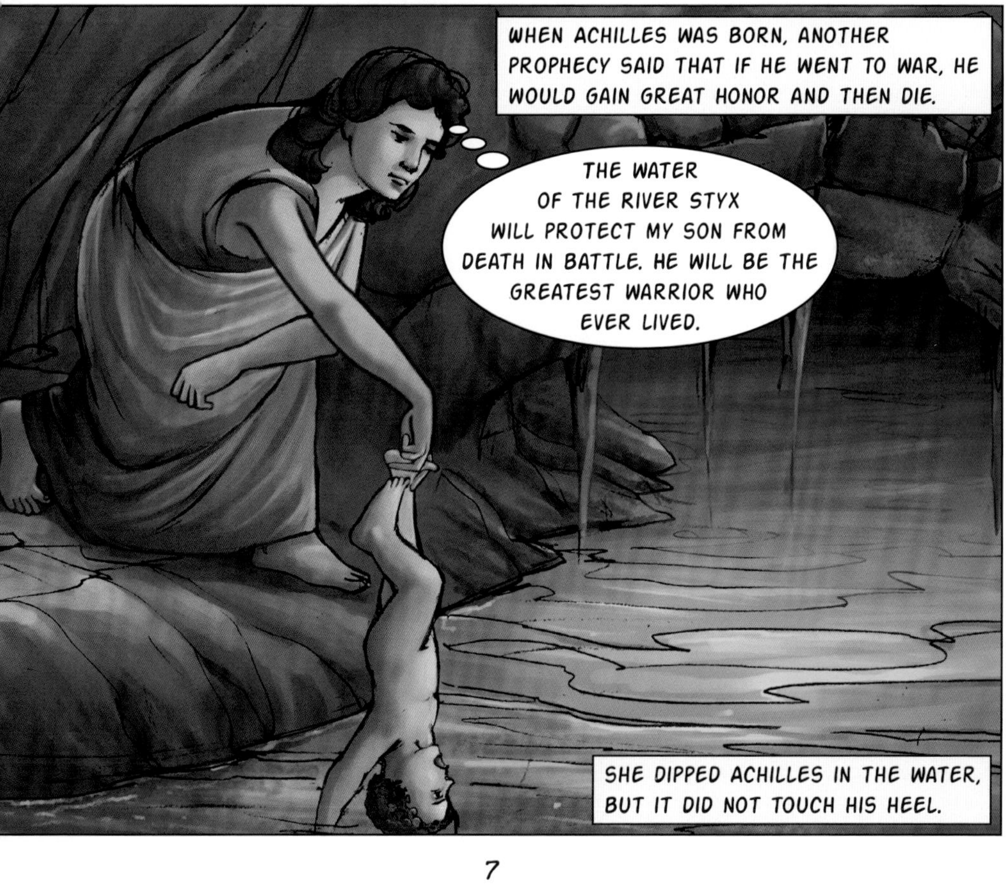
WHEN ACHILLES WAS BORN, ANOTHER PROPHECY SAID THAT IF HE WENT TO WAR, HE WOULD GAIN GREAT HONOR AND THEN DIE.
THE WATER OF THE RIVER STYX WILL PROTECT MY SON FROM DEATH IN BATTLE. HE WILL BE THE GREATEST WARRIOR WHO EVER LIVED.
SHE DIPPED ACHILLES IN THE WATER, BUT IT DID NOT TOUCH HIS HEEL.

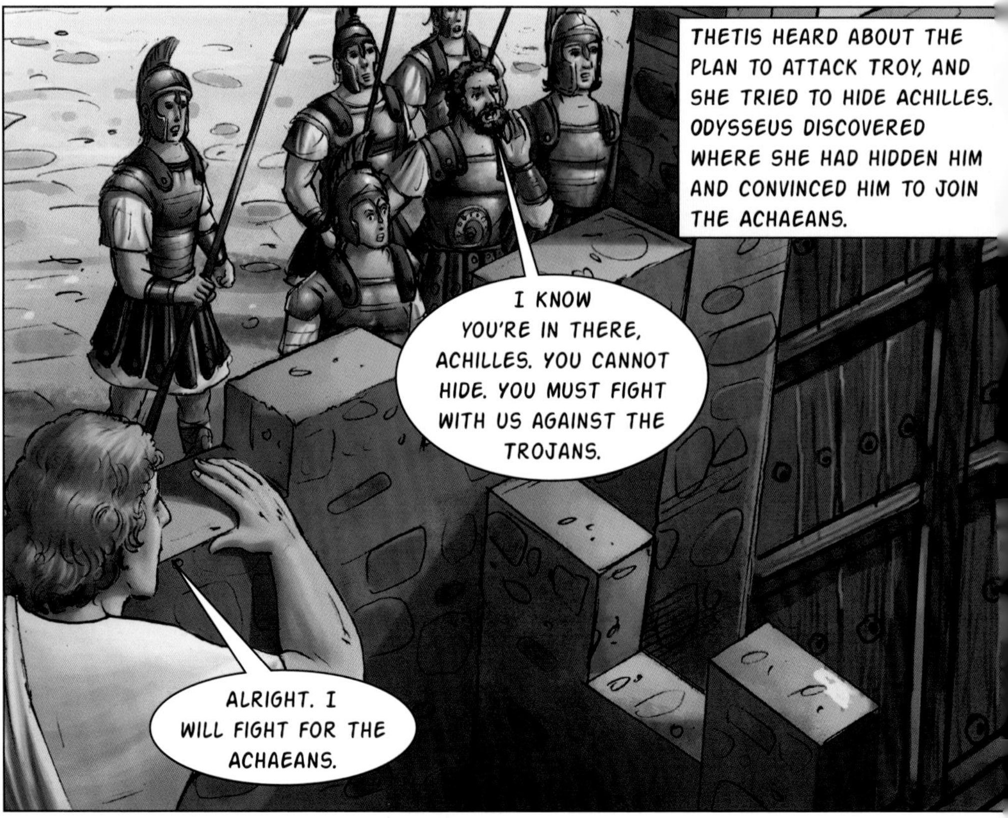
THETIS HEARD ABOUT THE PLAN TO ATTACK TROY, AND SHE TRIED TO HIDE ACHILLES. ODYSSEUS DISCOVERED WHERE SHE HAD HIDDEN HIM AND CONVINCED HIM TO JOIN THE ACHAEANS.
I KNOW YOU'RE IN THERE, ACHILLES. YOU CANNOT HIDE. YOU MUST FIGHT WITH US AGAINST THE TROJANS.
ALRIGHT. I WILL FIGHT FOR THE ACHAEANS.

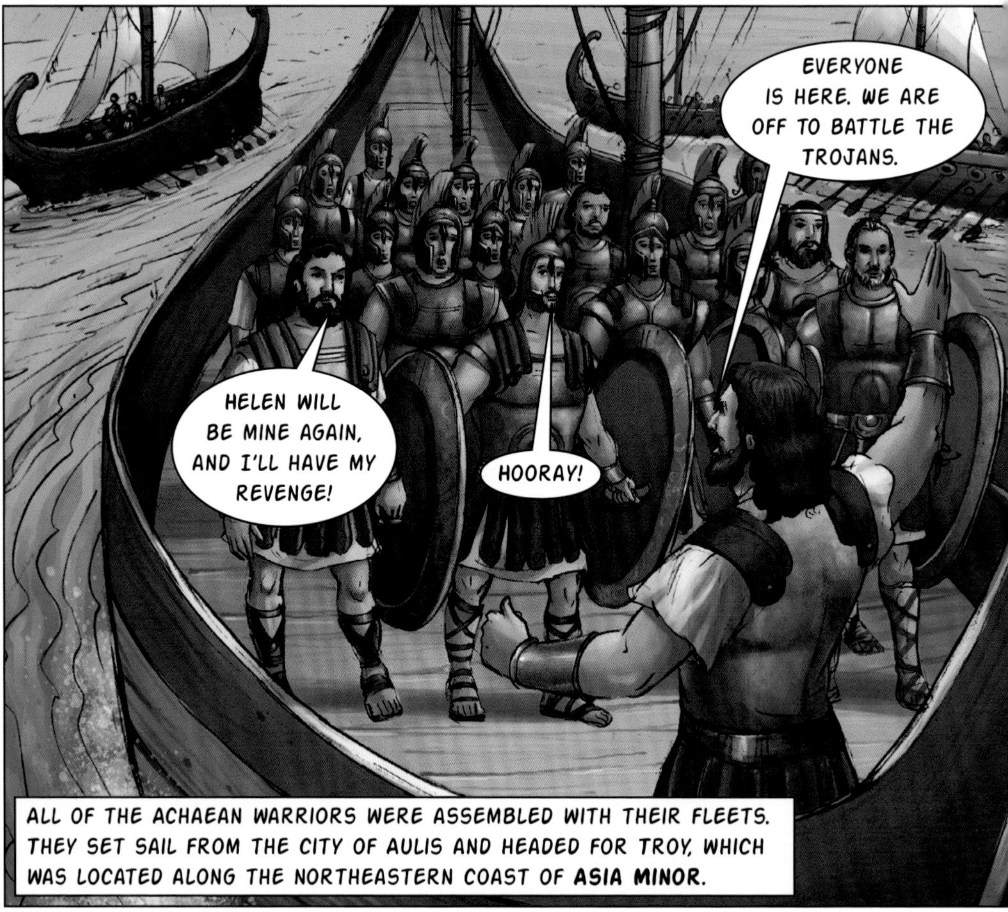
EVERYONE IS HERE. WE ARE OFF TO BATTLE THE TROJANS.
HELEN WILL BE MINE AGAIN, AND I'LL HAVE MY REVENGE!
HOORAY!
ALL OF THE ACHAEAN WARRIORS WERE ASSEMBLED WITH THEIR FLEETS. THEY SET SAIL FROM THE CITY OF AULIS AND HEADED FOR TROY, WHICH WAS LOCATED ALONG THE NORTHEASTERN COAST OF ASIA MINOR.

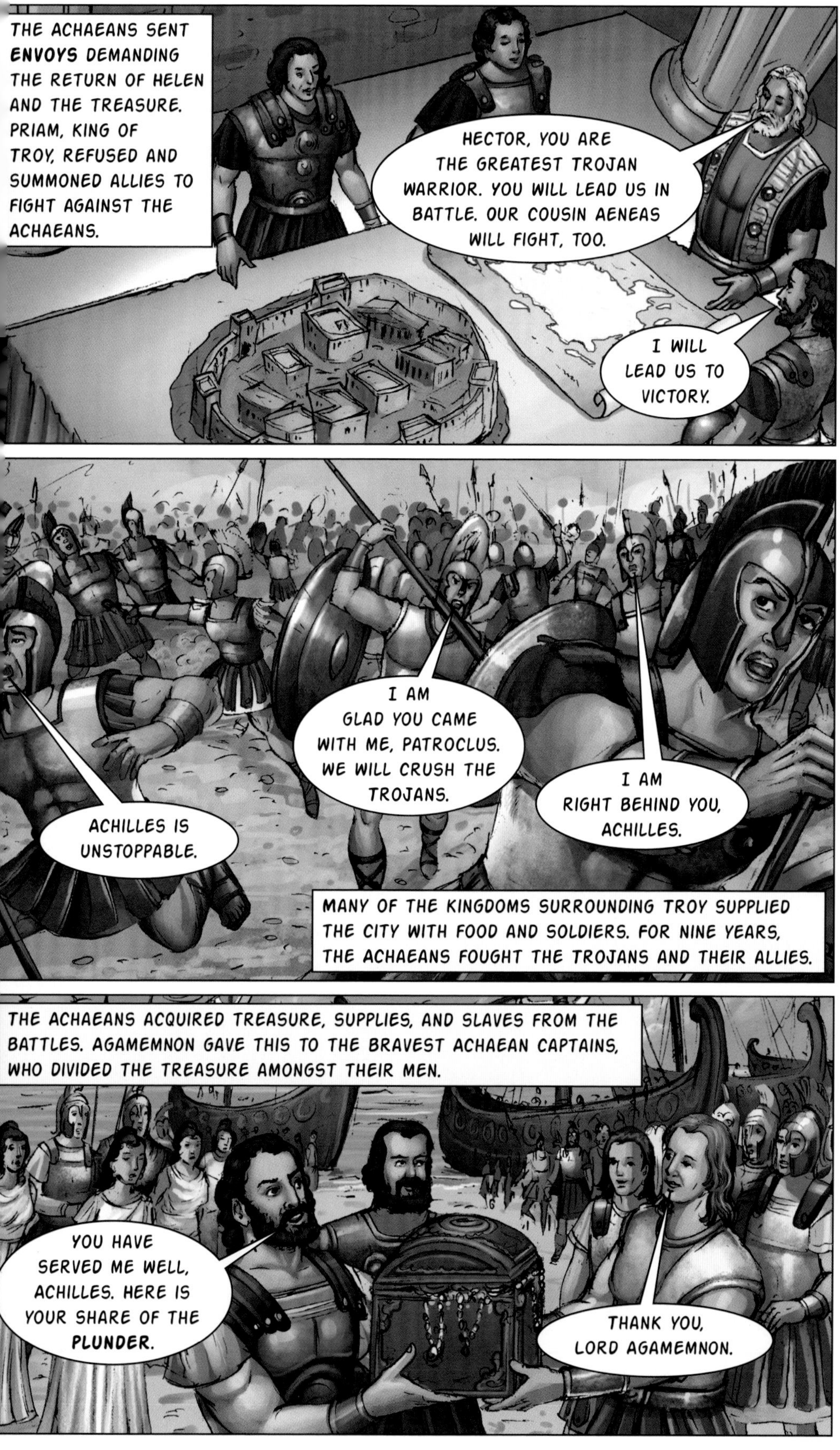
THE ACHAEANS SENT **ENVOYS** DEMANDING THE RETURN OF HELEN AND THE TREASURE. PRIAM, KING OF TROY, REFUSED AND SUMMONED ALLIES TO FIGHT AGAINST THE ACHAEANS.
HECTOR, YOU ARE THE GREATEST TROJAN WARRIOR. YOU WILL LEAD US IN BATTLE. OUR COUSIN AENEAS WILL FIGHT, TOO.
I WILL LEAD US TO VICTORY.
I AM GLAD YOU CAME WITH ME, PATROCLUS. WE WILL CRUSH THE TROJANS.
I AM RIGHT BEHIND YOU, ACHILLES.
ACHILLES IS UNSTOPPABLE.
MANY OF THE KINGDOMS SURROUNDING TROY SUPPLIED THE CITY WITH FOOD AND SOLDIERS. FOR NINE YEARS, THE ACHAEANS FOUGHT THE TROJANS AND THEIR ALLIES.
THE ACHAEANS ACQUIRED TREASURE, SUPPLIES, AND SLAVES FROM THE BATTLES. AGAMEMNON GAVE THIS TO THE BRAVEST ACHAEAN CAPTAINS, WHO DIVIDED THE TREASURE AMONGST THEIR MEN.
YOU HAVE SERVED ME WELL, ACHILLES. HERE IS YOUR SHARE OF THE **PLUNDER**.
THANK YOU, LORD AGAMEMNON.

IN THE TENTH YEAR OF THE WAR, THE ACHAEANS BESIEGED THE CITY OF TROY. THEY BEACHED THEIR SHIPS AND BUILT A WALL AND A DITCH AS A DEFENSE AGAINST THE TROJANS.

THE FIGHTING DID NOT GO WELL, HOWEVER. A **PLAGUE** BROKE OUT IN THE ACHAEAN CAMP.

THE ACHAEANS ASKED THE GODS HOW TO GET RID OF THE PLAGUE. THE SEER CALCHAS TOLD THEM WHAT TO DO.

AGAMEMNON, YOU HAVE TAKEN CHRYSEIS AS YOUR SLAVE. SHE IS THE DAUGHTER OF THE PRIEST OF APOLLO. NOW APOLLO IS ANGRY. YOU MUST RETURN HER TO GET RID OF THE PLAGUE.

HOW DARE HE SAY THIS TO ME!

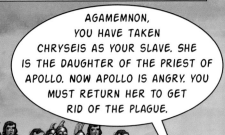

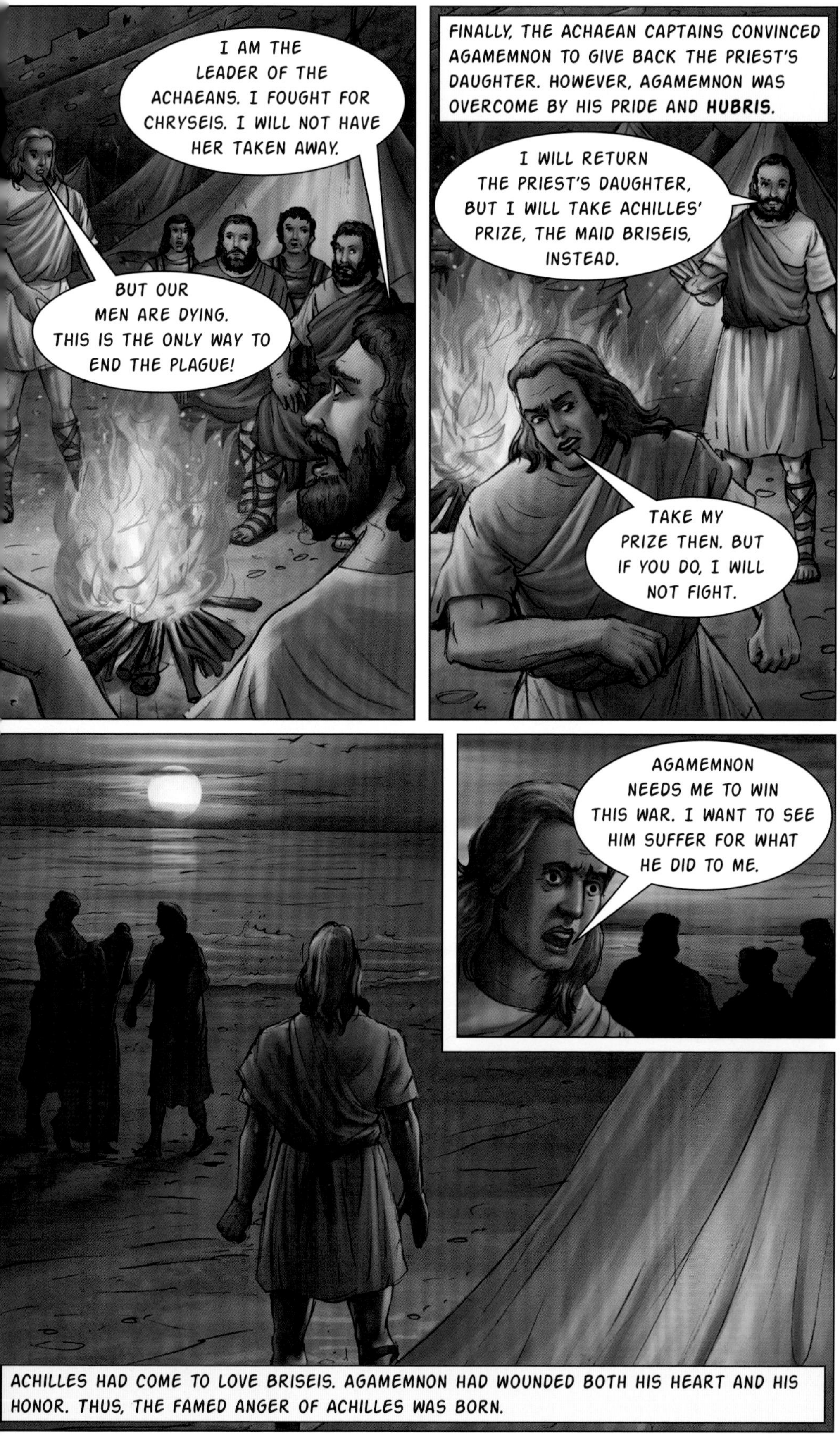
I AM THE LEADER OF THE ACHAEANS. I FOUGHT FOR CHRYSEIS. I WILL NOT HAVE HER TAKEN AWAY.
BUT OUR MEN ARE DYING. THIS IS THE ONLY WAY TO END THE PLAGUE!
FINALLY, THE ACHAEAN CAPTAINS CONVINCED AGAMEMNON TO GIVE BACK THE PRIEST'S DAUGHTER. HOWEVER, AGAMEMNON WAS OVERCOME BY HIS PRIDE AND **HUBRIS**.
I WILL RETURN THE PRIEST'S DAUGHTER, BUT I WILL TAKE ACHILLES' PRIZE, THE MAID BRISEIS, INSTEAD.
TAKE MY PRIZE THEN. BUT IF YOU DO, I WILL NOT FIGHT.
AGAMEMNON NEEDS ME TO WIN THIS WAR. I WANT TO SEE HIM SUFFER FOR WHAT HE DID TO ME.
ACHILLES HAD COME TO LOVE BRISEIS. AGAMEMNON HAD WOUNDED BOTH HIS HEART AND HIS HONOR. THUS, THE FAMED ANGER OF ACHILLES WAS BORN.

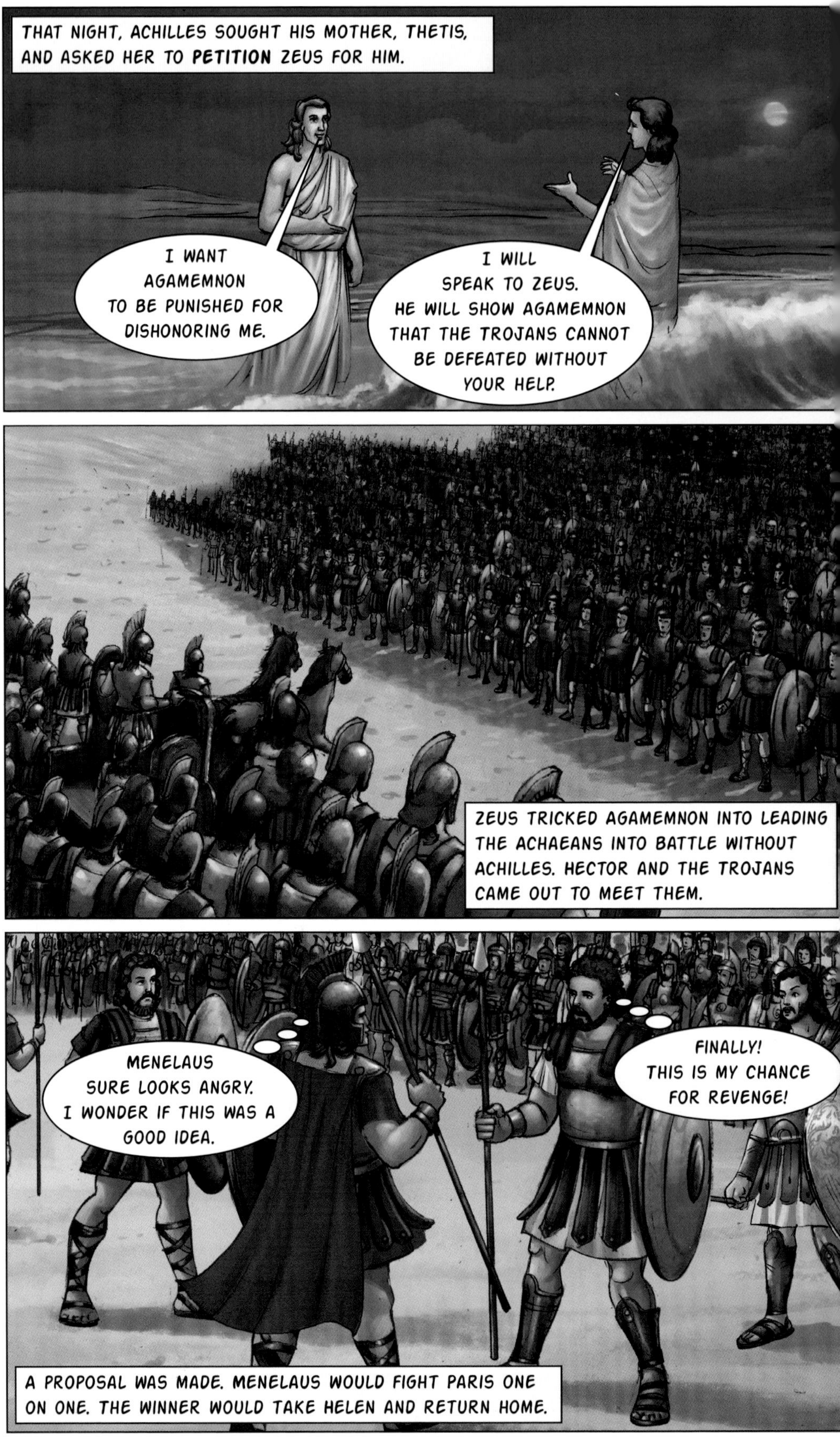
THAT NIGHT, ACHILLES SOUGHT HIS MOTHER, THETIS, AND ASKED HER TO **PETITION** ZEUS FOR HIM.
I WANT AGAMEMNON TO BE PUNISHED FOR DISHONORING ME.
I WILL SPEAK TO ZEUS. HE WILL SHOW AGAMEMNON THAT THE TROJANS CANNOT BE DEFEATED WITHOUT YOUR HELP.
ZEUS TRICKED AGAMEMNON INTO LEADING THE ACHAEANS INTO BATTLE WITHOUT ACHILLES. HECTOR AND THE TROJANS CAME OUT TO MEET THEM.
MENELAUS SURE LOOKS ANGRY. I WONDER IF THIS WAS A GOOD IDEA.
FINALLY! THIS IS MY CHANCE FOR REVENGE!
A PROPOSAL WAS MADE. MENELAUS WOULD FIGHT PARIS ONE ON ONE. THE WINNER WOULD TAKE HELEN AND RETURN HOME.

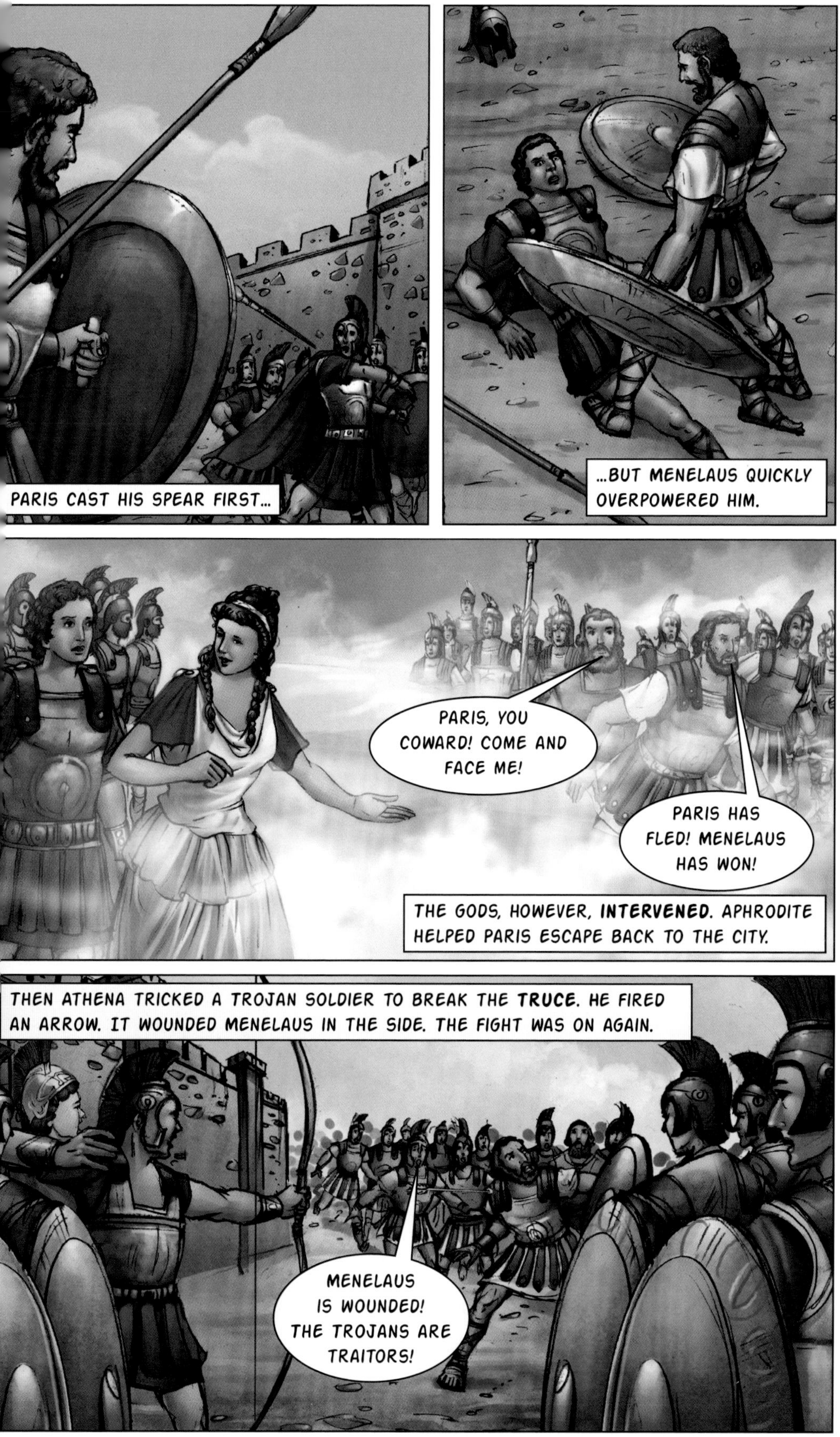
PARIS CAST HIS SPEAR FIRST...
...BUT MENELAUS QUICKLY OVERPOWERED HIM.
PARIS, YOU COWARD! COME AND FACE ME!
PARIS HAS FLED! MENELAUS HAS WON!
THE GODS, HOWEVER, **INTERVENED**. APHRODITE HELPED PARIS ESCAPE BACK TO THE CITY.
THEN ATHENA TRICKED A TROJAN SOLDIER TO BREAK THE **TRUCE**. HE FIRED AN ARROW. IT WOUNDED MENELAUS IN THE SIDE. THE FIGHT WAS ON AGAIN.
MENELAUS IS WOUNDED! THE TROJANS ARE TRAITORS!

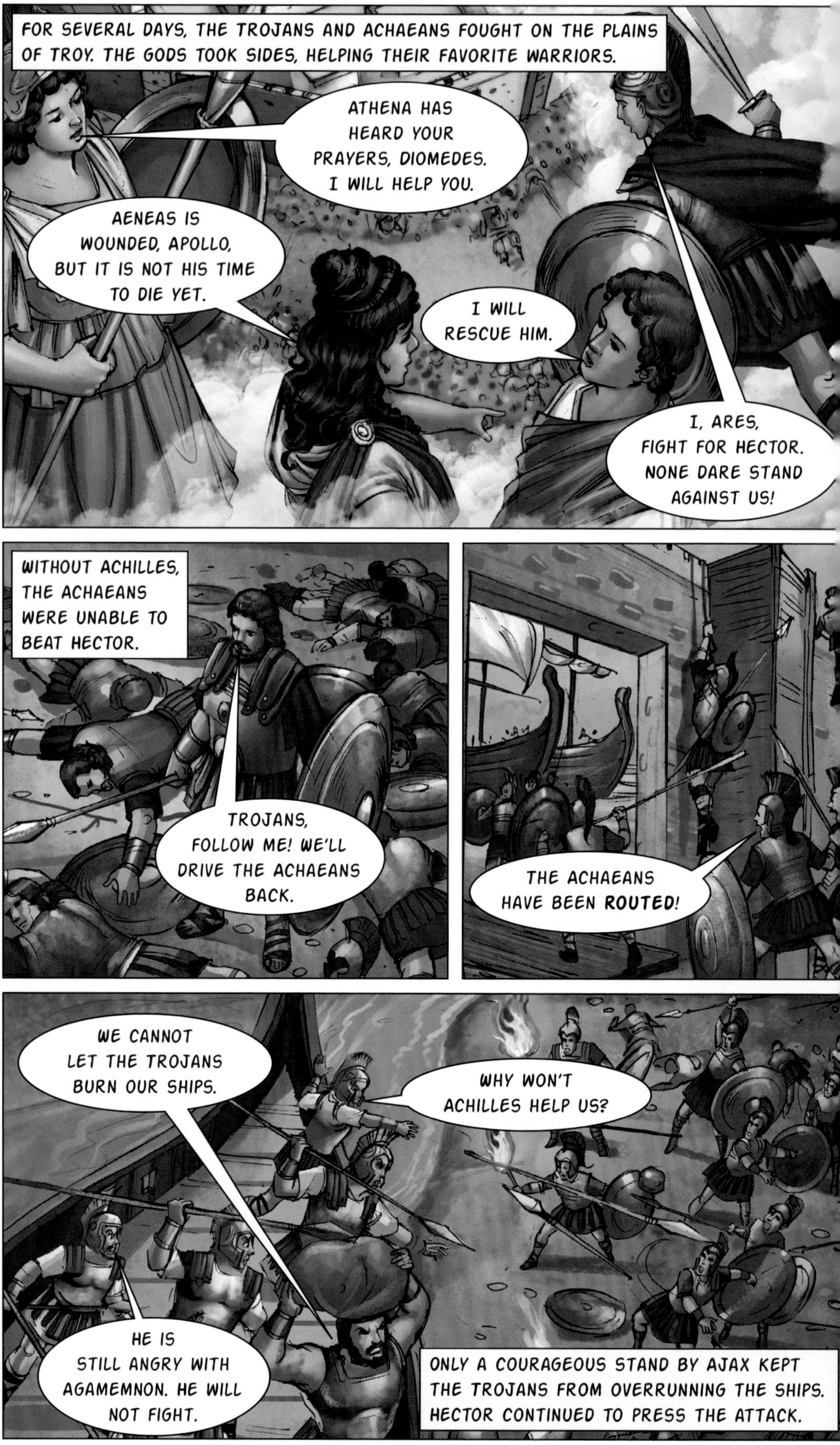
FOR SEVERAL DAYS, THE TROJANS AND ACHAEANS FOUGHT ON THE PLAINS OF TROY. THE GODS TOOK SIDES, HELPING THEIR FAVORITE WARRIORS.
ATHENA HAS HEARD YOUR PRAYERS, DIOMEDES. I WILL HELP YOU.
AENEAS IS WOUNDED, APOLLO, BUT IT IS NOT HIS TIME TO DIE YET.
I WILL RESCUE HIM.
I, ARES, FIGHT FOR HECTOR. NONE DARE STAND AGAINST US!
WITHOUT ACHILLES, THE ACHAEANS WERE UNABLE TO BEAT HECTOR.
TROJANS, FOLLOW ME! WE'LL DRIVE THE ACHAEANS BACK.
THE ACHAEANS HAVE BEEN **ROUTED**!
WE CANNOT LET THE TROJANS BURN OUR SHIPS.
WHY WON'T ACHILLES HELP US?
HE IS STILL ANGRY WITH AGAMEMNON. HE WILL NOT FIGHT.
ONLY A COURAGEOUS STAND BY AJAX KEPT THE TROJANS FROM OVERRUNNING THE SHIPS. HECTOR CONTINUED TO PRESS THE ATTACK.

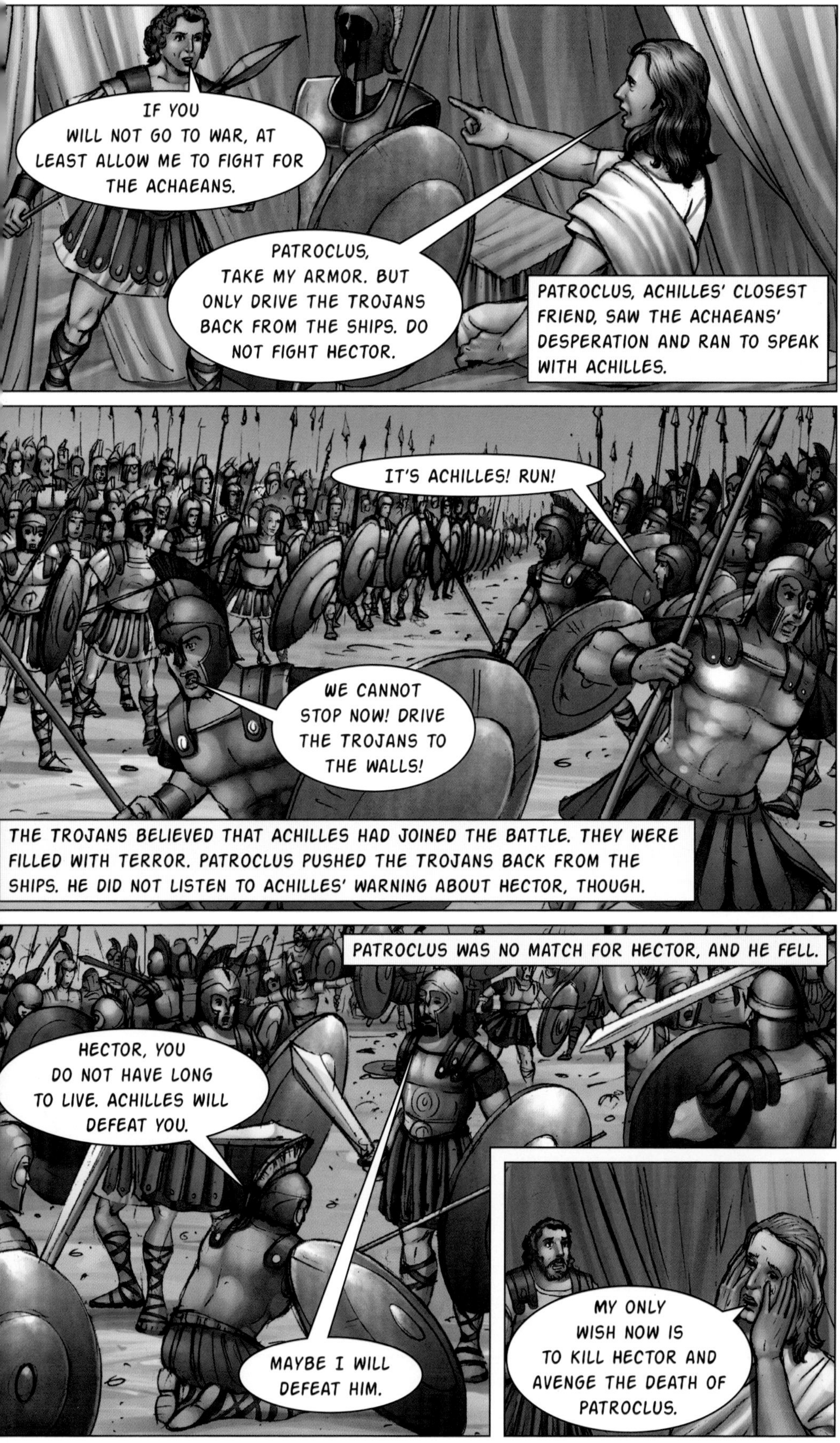
IF YOU WILL NOT GO TO WAR, AT LEAST ALLOW ME TO FIGHT FOR THE ACHAEANS.
PATROCLUS, TAKE MY ARMOR. BUT ONLY DRIVE THE TROJANS BACK FROM THE SHIPS. DO NOT FIGHT HECTOR.
PATROCLUS, ACHILLES' CLOSEST FRIEND, SAW THE ACHAEANS' DESPERATION AND RAN TO SPEAK WITH ACHILLES.
IT'S ACHILLES! RUN!
WE CANNOT STOP NOW! DRIVE THE TROJANS TO THE WALLS!
THE TROJANS BELIEVED THAT ACHILLES HAD JOINED THE BATTLE. THEY WERE FILLED WITH TERROR. PATROCLUS PUSHED THE TROJANS BACK FROM THE SHIPS. HE DID NOT LISTEN TO ACHILLES' WARNING ABOUT HECTOR, THOUGH.
PATROCLUS WAS NO MATCH FOR HECTOR, AND HE FELL.
HECTOR, YOU DO NOT HAVE LONG TO LIVE. ACHILLES WILL DEFEAT YOU.
MAYBE I WILL DEFEAT HIM.
MY ONLY WISH NOW IS TO KILL HECTOR AND AVENGE THE DEATH OF PATROCLUS.

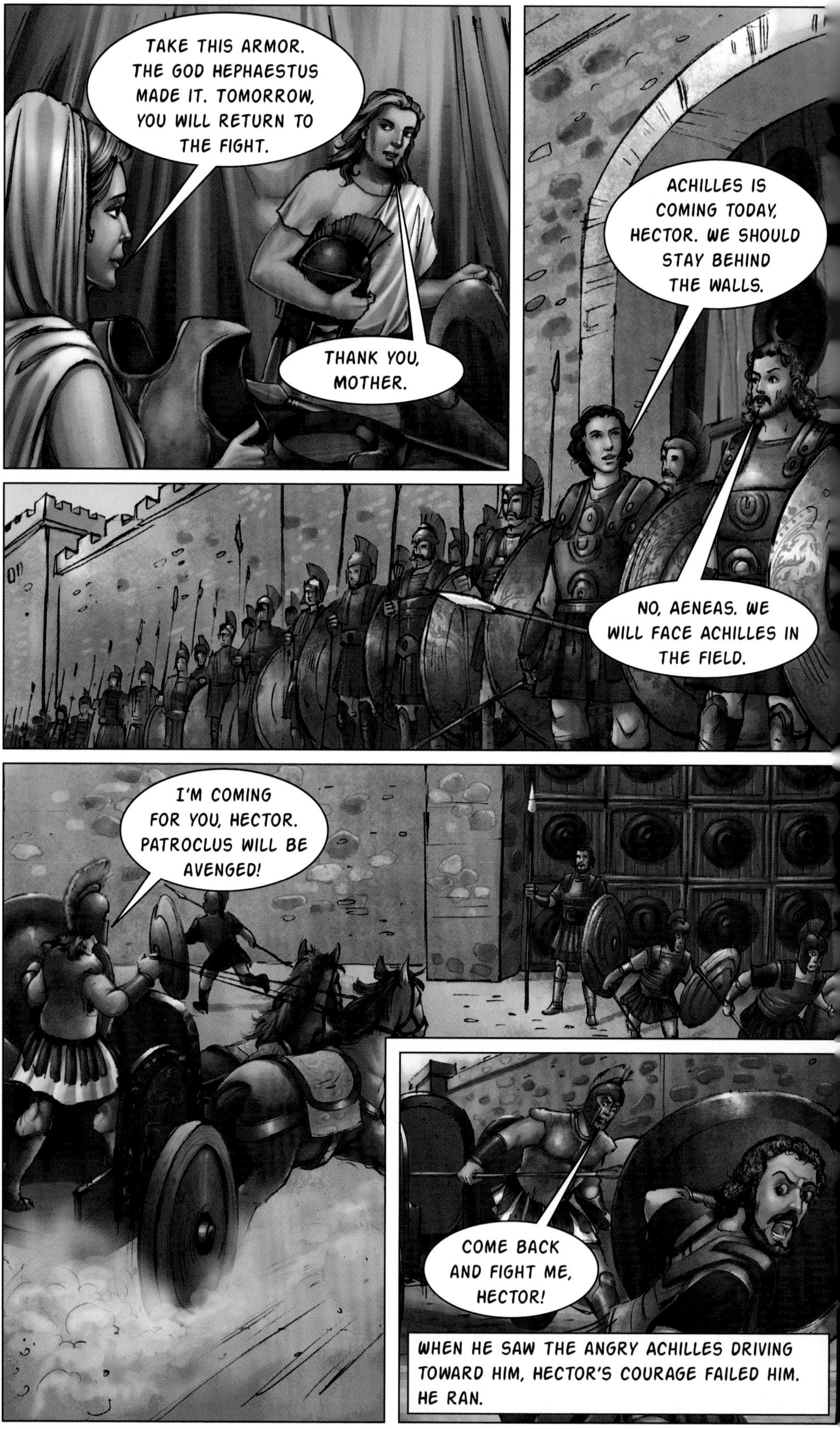
TAKE THIS ARMOR. THE GOD HEPHAESTUS MADE IT. TOMORROW, YOU WILL RETURN TO THE FIGHT.
THANK YOU, MOTHER.
ACHILLES IS COMING TODAY, HECTOR. WE SHOULD STAY BEHIND THE WALLS.
NO, AENEAS. WE WILL FACE ACHILLES IN THE FIELD.
I'M COMING FOR YOU, HECTOR. PATROCLUS WILL BE AVENGED!
COME BACK AND FIGHT ME, HECTOR!
WHEN HE SAW THE ANGRY ACHILLES DRIVING TOWARD HIM, HECTOR'S COURAGE FAILED HIM. HE RAN.

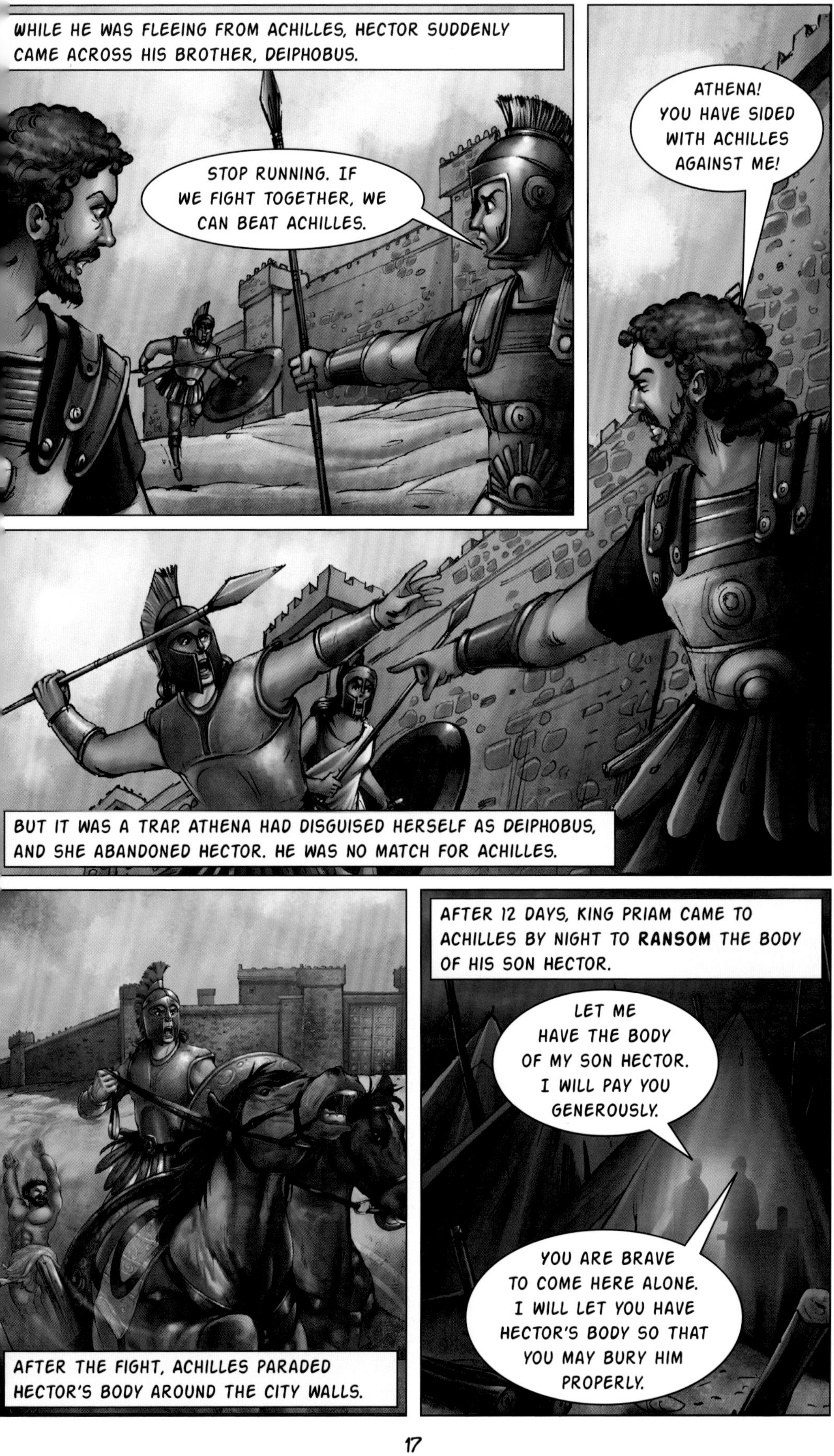

WHILE HE WAS FLEEING FROM ACHILLES, HECTOR SUDDENLY CAME ACROSS HIS BROTHER, DEIPHOBUS.
STOP RUNNING. IF WE FIGHT TOGETHER, WE CAN BEAT ACHILLES.
ATHENA! YOU HAVE SIDED WITH ACHILLES AGAINST ME!
BUT IT WAS A TRAP. ATHENA HAD DISGUISED HERSELF AS DEIPHOBUS, AND SHE ABANDONED HECTOR. HE WAS NO MATCH FOR ACHILLES.
AFTER THE FIGHT, ACHILLES PARADED HECTOR'S BODY AROUND THE CITY WALLS.
AFTER 12 DAYS, KING PRIAM CAME TO ACHILLES BY NIGHT TO **RANSOM** THE BODY OF HIS SON HECTOR.
LET ME HAVE THE BODY OF MY SON HECTOR. I WILL PAY YOU GENEROUSLY.
YOU ARE BRAVE TO COME HERE ALONE. I WILL LET YOU HAVE HECTOR'S BODY SO THAT YOU MAY BURY HIM PROPERLY.

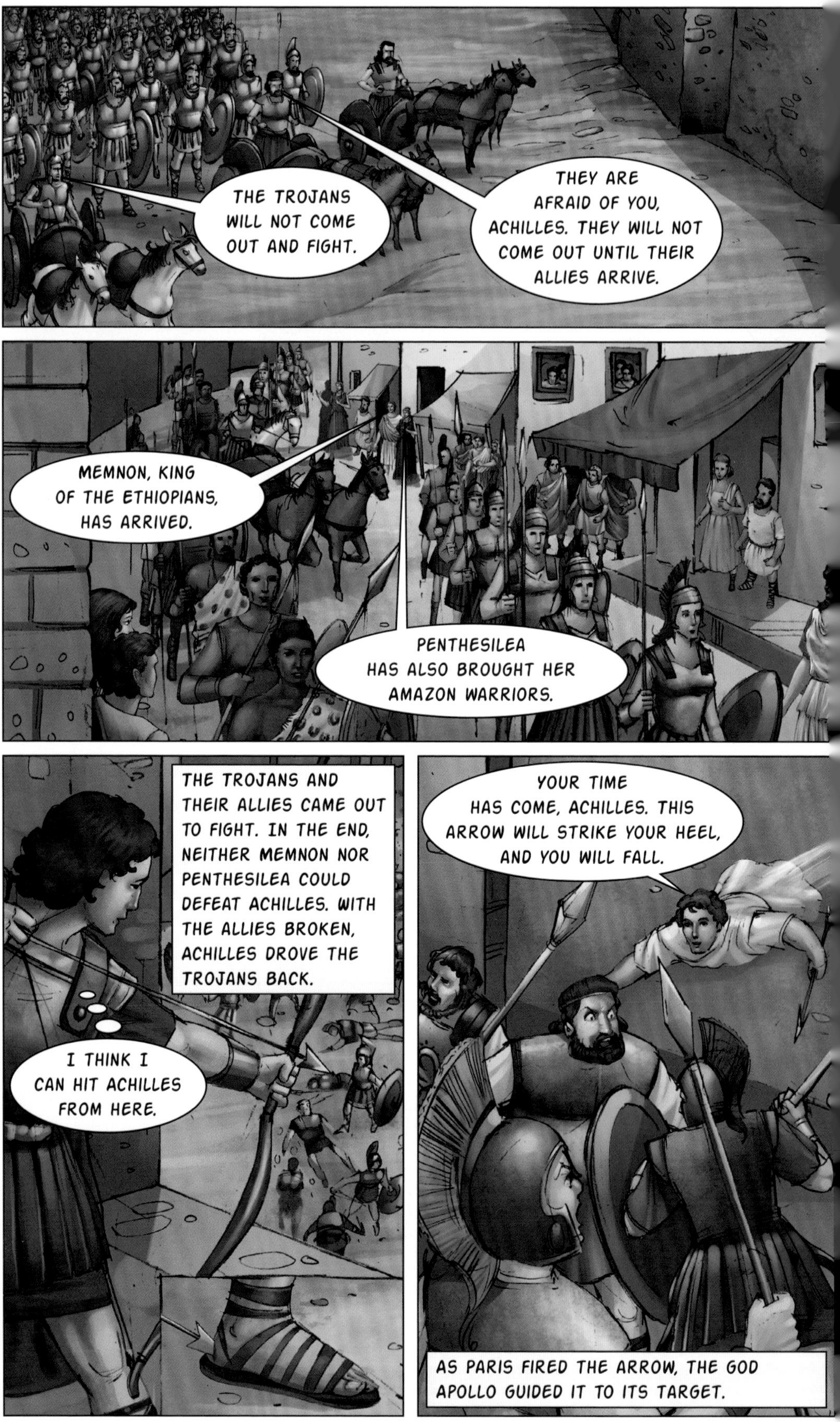
THE TROJANS WILL NOT COME OUT AND FIGHT.
THEY ARE AFRAID OF YOU, ACHILLES. THEY WILL NOT COME OUT UNTIL THEIR ALLIES ARRIVE.
MEMNON, KING OF THE ETHIOPIANS, HAS ARRIVED.
PENTHESILEA HAS ALSO BROUGHT HER AMAZON WARRIORS.
THE TROJANS AND THEIR ALLIES CAME OUT TO FIGHT. IN THE END, NEITHER MEMNON NOR PENTHESILEA COULD DEFEAT ACHILLES. WITH THE ALLIES BROKEN, ACHILLES DROVE THE TROJANS BACK.
I THINK I CAN HIT ACHILLES FROM HERE.
YOUR TIME HAS COME, ACHILLES. THIS ARROW WILL STRIKE YOUR HEEL, AND YOU WILL FALL.
AS PARIS FIRED THE ARROW, THE GOD APOLLO GUIDED IT TO ITS TARGET.

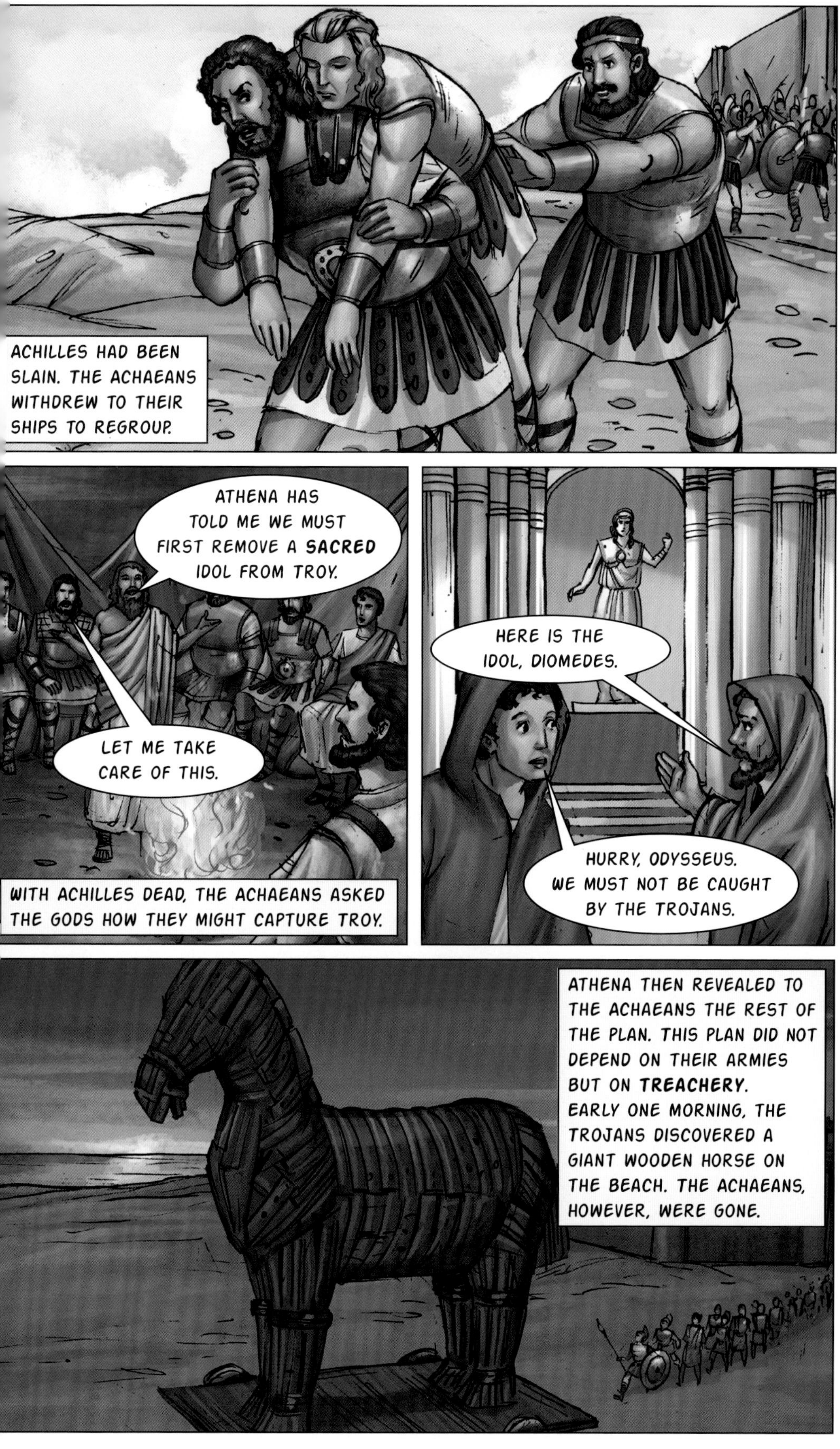
ACHILLES HAD BEEN SLAIN. THE ACHAEANS WITHDREW TO THEIR SHIPS TO REGROUP.
ATHENA HAS TOLD ME WE MUST FIRST REMOVE A **SACRED** IDOL FROM TROY.
LET ME TAKE CARE OF THIS.
WITH ACHILLES DEAD, THE ACHAEANS ASKED THE GODS HOW THEY MIGHT CAPTURE TROY.
HERE IS THE IDOL, DIOMEDES.
HURRY, ODYSSEUS. WE MUST NOT BE CAUGHT BY THE TROJANS.
ATHENA THEN REVEALED TO THE ACHAEANS THE REST OF THE PLAN. THIS PLAN DID NOT DEPEND ON THEIR ARMIES BUT ON **TREACHERY**. EARLY ONE MORNING, THE TROJANS DISCOVERED A GIANT WOODEN HORSE ON THE BEACH. THE ACHAEANS, HOWEVER, WERE GONE.

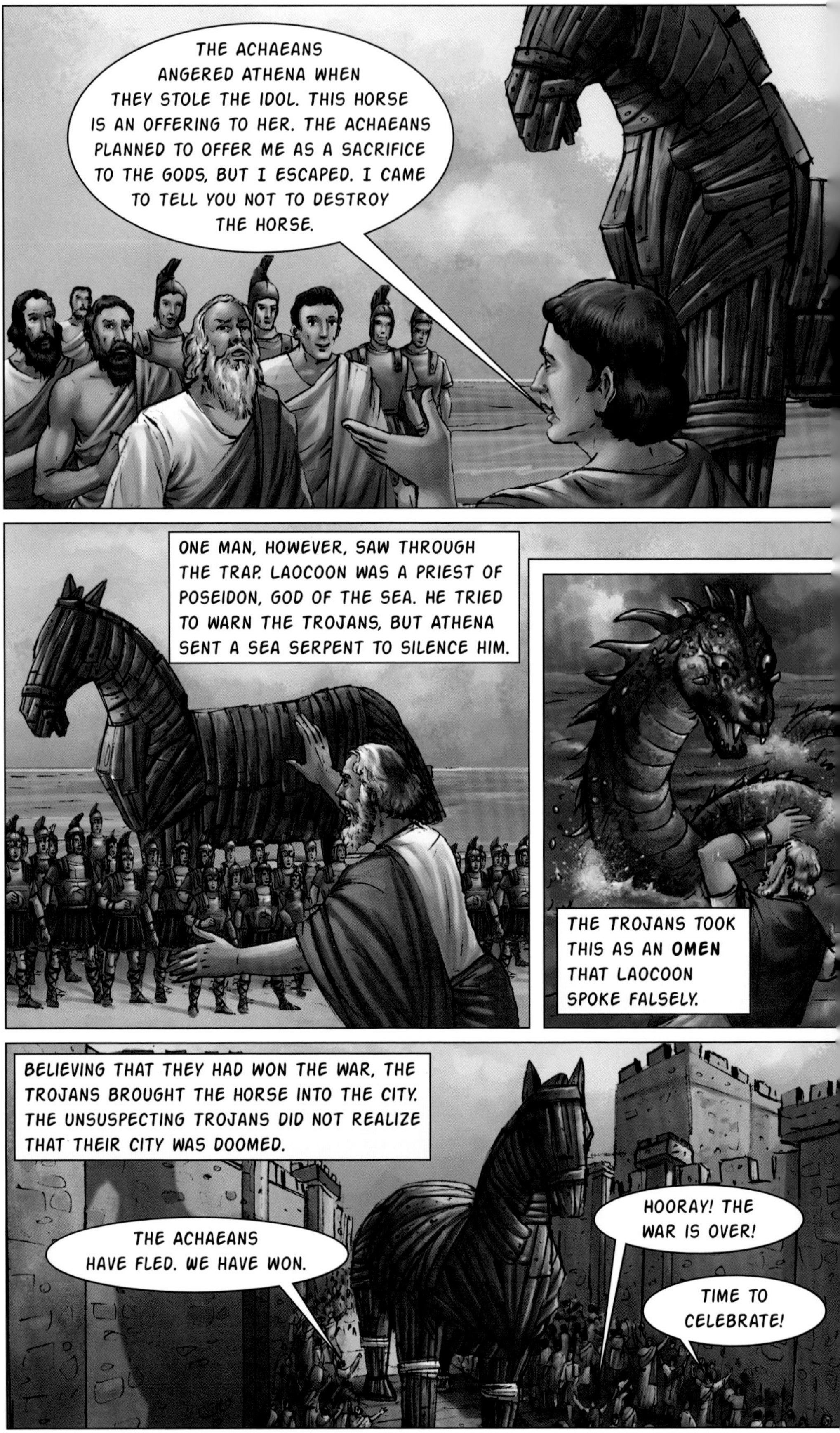
THE ACHAEANS ANGERED ATHENA WHEN THEY STOLE THE IDOL. THIS HORSE IS AN OFFERING TO HER. THE ACHAEANS PLANNED TO OFFER ME AS A SACRIFICE TO THE GODS, BUT I ESCAPED. I CAME TO TELL YOU NOT TO DESTROY THE HORSE.
ONE MAN, HOWEVER, SAW THROUGH THE TRAP. LAOCOON WAS A PRIEST OF POSEIDON, GOD OF THE SEA. HE TRIED TO WARN THE TROJANS, BUT ATHENA SENT A SEA SERPENT TO SILENCE HIM.
THE TROJANS TOOK THIS AS AN **OMEN** THAT LAOCOON SPOKE FALSELY.
BELIEVING THAT THEY HAD WON THE WAR, THE TROJANS BROUGHT THE HORSE INTO THE CITY. THE UNSUSPECTING TROJANS DID NOT REALIZE THAT THEIR CITY WAS DOOMED.
THE ACHAEANS HAVE FLED. WE HAVE WON.
HOORAY! THE WAR IS OVER!
TIME TO CELEBRATE!

A SMALL GROUP OF ACHAEAN SOLDIERS, LED BY ODYSSEUS, MENELAUS, AND DIOMEDES, WERE HIDDEN INSIDE THE HORSE.
THE SOLDIERS OPENED THE GATES, AND THE ACHAEAN ARMIES POURED IN. THE TROJANS WERE DEFENSELESS. THAT NIGHT, THE CITY FELL.
PRIAM
AJAX
AGAMEMNON
PARIS
HECTOR
MANY HEROES **PERISHED** IN THE WAR. PHILOCTETES KILLED PARIS. PRIAM DIED WHEN THE CITY FELL. AJAX WENT MAD AND KILLED HIMSELF. WHEN AGAMEMNON RETURNED HOME, HE WAS MURDERED BY HIS WIFE.
HELEN AND MENELAUS WERE REUNITED, AND THEY RETURNED HOME TO SPARTA.
FINALLY, WE ARE HOME.
ODYSSEUS SET OUT TO RETURN TO HIS HOME IN ITHACA. HIS JOURNEY, HOWEVER, WOULD TAKE 10 MORE YEARS. BUT THAT IS A TALE FOR ANOTHER TIME.

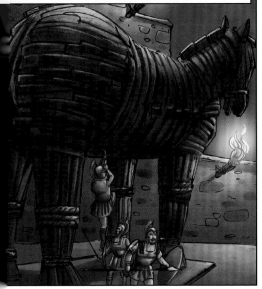

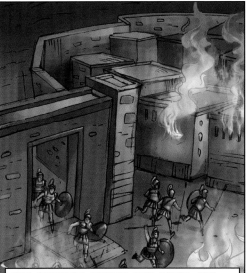

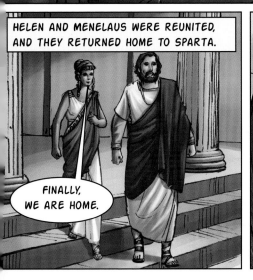

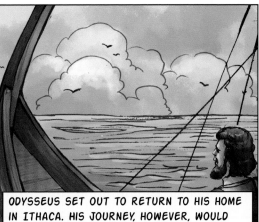

The Story of the Trojan War

The most famous accounts of the Trojan War can be found in the *Iliad,* by the Greek poet Homer. Little is known about Homer, including when he wrote. The historian Herodotus places him around 850 BC. In addition to Homer, many other ancient writers offered their versions of the Trojan War. The *Bibliotheca*, written by the mysterious author known as Pseudo-Apollodorus, covers a wide range of Greek myths related to the war. In addition, Greek playwrights wrote dramas that are centered on individual characters from the Trojan War. For example, the play *Agamemnon*, written by Aeschylus, picks up the story when Agamemnon returns home from the war. Sophocles play *Ajax* tells us how that hero went mad, leading to his death. These are only a few of the many stories and mysteries surrounding the Trojan War and the warriors who fought in it.

The World of Homer

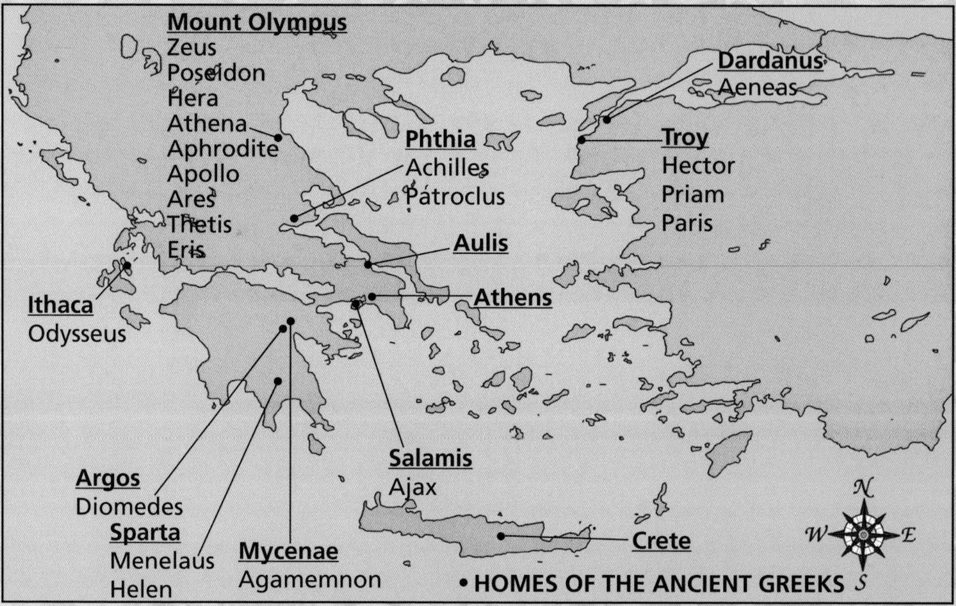
Mount Olympus
Zeus
Poseidon
Hera
Athena
Aphrodite
Apollo
Ares
Thetis
Eris
Dardanus
Aeneas
Phthia
Achilles
Patroclus
Troy
Hector
Priam
Paris
Aulis
Athens
Ithaca
Odysseus
Salamis
Ajax
Argos
Diomedes
Sparta
Menelaus
Helen
Mycenae
Agamemnon
Crete
N
W
E
S
• HOMES OF THE ANCIENT GREEKS

Glossary

abductor (ab-DUKT-ur) Someone who takes someone else away by force.

Achaean (uh-KEE-un) Having to do with Achaea, the region of Greece.

Asia Minor (AY-zhuh MY-nur) A region composed primarily of what is now modern-day Turkey.

avenged (uh-VENJD) Sought to punish one who has wronged you.

discord (DIS-kord) Disagreement and fighting.

envoys (ON-voyz) Representatives from one government to another.

hubris (HYOO-brus) Too much pride or self-confidence.

intervened (in-ter-VEEND) Interfered in someone else's affairs.

omen (OH-men) Something believed to predict the future.

perished (PER-ishd) Were destroyed or killed.

petition (puh-TIH-shun) A formal way to ask for something to be done.

plague (PLAYG) A very bad illness, curse, or hardship.

plunder (PLUN-der) Something taken by force.

prophecy (PRAH-fe-see) A statement that something will happen in the future.

ransom (RAN-sum) To ask for money or goods to free a captive.

routed (ROWT-ed) Badly defeated and forced to retreat quickly.

sacred (SAY-kred) Blessed; highly respected and considered very important.

treachery (TREH-chuh-ree) Being false, faithless, or dangerous.

Trojan (TROH-jun) A native of Troy.

truce (TROOS) An agreement to end a battle or a war.

Index

Websites

Due to the changing nature of Internet links, PowerKids Press has developed an online list of websites related to the subject of this book. This site is updated regularly. Please use this link to access the list:

www.powerkidslinks.com/grmy/achill